take it apart

SPACE SHUTTLE

By Chris Oxlade

Illustrated by Mike Grey

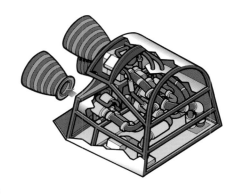
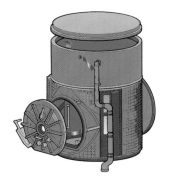
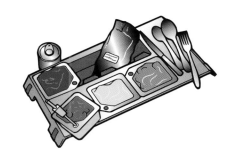

Thameside Press

Distributed in the United States by
Smart Apple Media
1980 Lookout Drive
North Mankato, MN 56003

Text copyright © Chris Oxlade
Illustrator copyright © Mike Grey

ISBN 1-930643-97-7

Library of Congress Control Number 2002 141351

Editor: Veronica Ross
Designer: Guy Callaby
Researcher: Susie Brooks
Illustrator: Mike Grey
Consultants: Elizabeth Atkinson and Robin Kerrod

Printed by South China Printing Co. Ltd., Hong Kong

Inside This Book

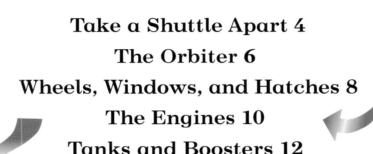

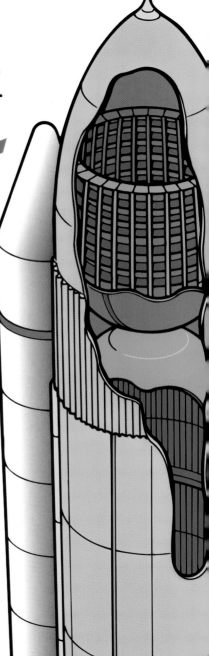

Take a Shuttle Apart 4

The Orbiter 6

Wheels, Windows, and Hatches 8

The Engines 10

Tanks and Boosters 12

The Flight Deck 14

The Living Quarters 16

Eating and Drinking 18

Inside the Payload Bay 20

Spacelab 22

The Robot Arm 24

Working Outside 26

Ready to Launch 28

Useful Words 30

Index 32

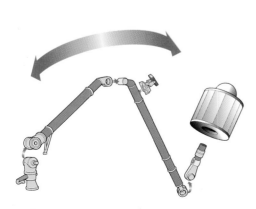

Take a Shuttle Apart

● A space shuttle can go into space many times. It takes off like a rocket and lands like a glider.

● A shuttle has thousands of parts. They are made of metal, plastic, glass, and other materials.

● A shuttle has three main pieces – the orbiter, the external fuel tank, and the rocket boosters.

● This book shows you the main parts of a space shuttle and how they fit together.

Fact Box
On its launch pad, ready for liftoff, a space shuttle stands 184 feet high. That's as tall as a 15-story building.

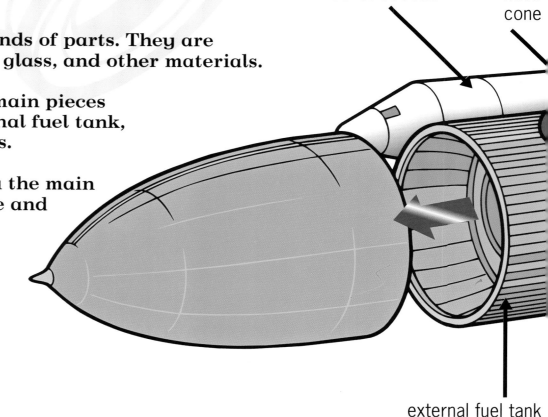

rocket booster

nose cone

external fuel tank

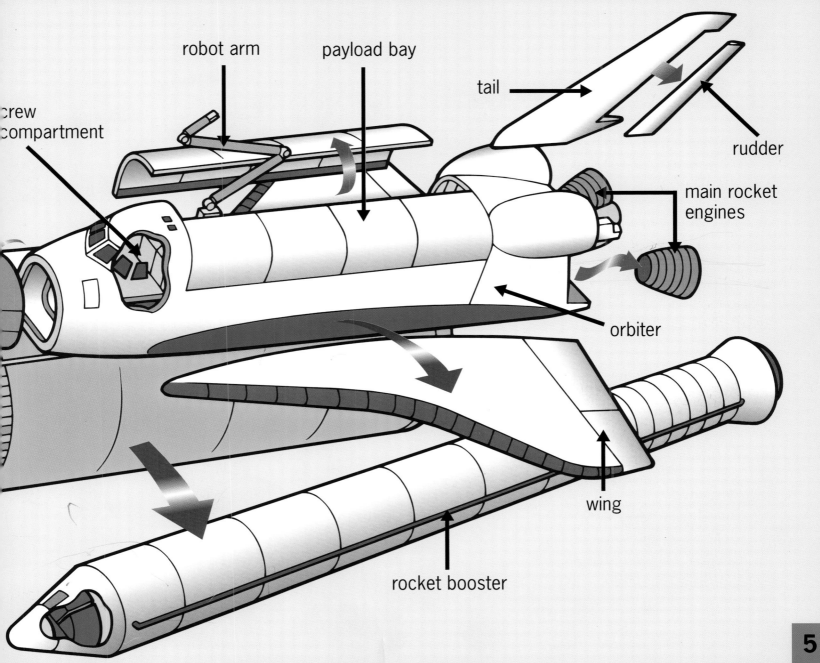

robot arm

payload bay

crew
compartment

tail

rudder

main rocket
engines

orbiter

wing

rocket booster

5

The Orbiter

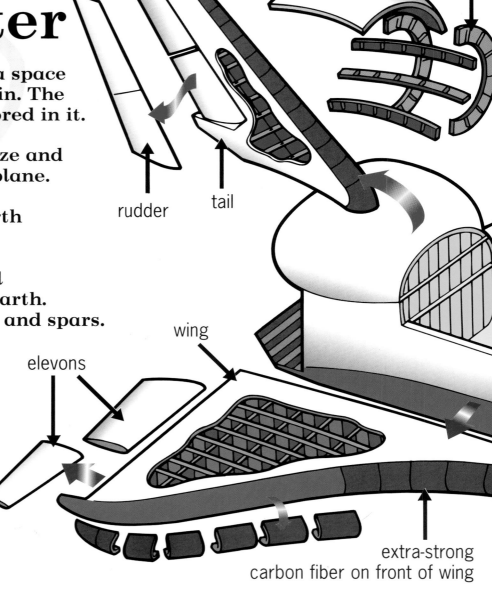

- The orbiter is the part of a space shuttle that the crew travel in. The payload, or cargo, is also stored in it.

- The orbiter is about the size and shape of a small passenger plane.

- The orbiter returns to Earth after a mission.

- The wings and tail control the orbiter as it returns to Earth. They are made of metal ribs and spars.

Fact Box
There are more than 21,000 tiles on the orbiter. Each one must be a slightly different shape from the others.

metal skin

metal ri
and spa

rudder

tail

wing

elevons

extra-strong
carbon fiber on front of wing

Terrific tiles

The orbiter is covered in special ceramic tiles. When it returns to Earth, the outside of the orbiter gets very hot. The tiles protect it from the heat.

On the back of the wings are moving flaps called elevons. There is another flap called a rudder on the back of the tail. The pilot uses the elevons and rudder to steer the orbiter as it glides back to Earth.

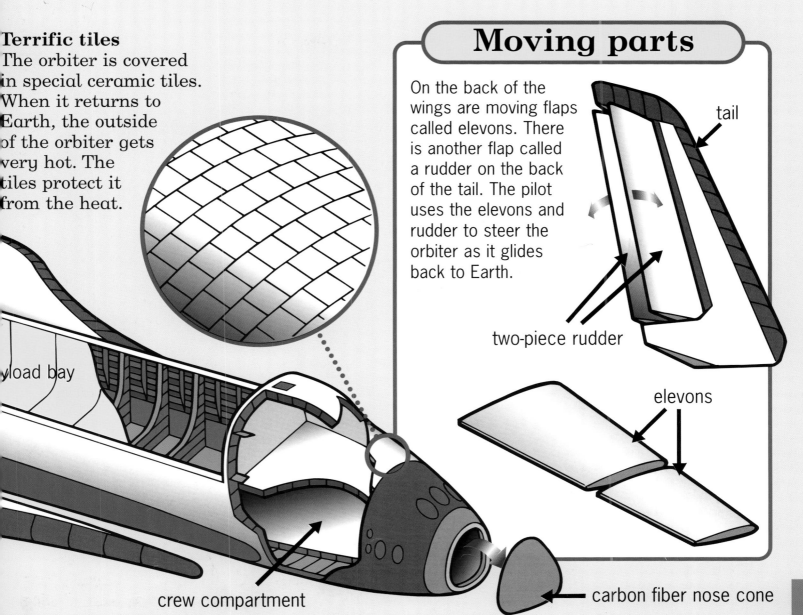

tail

two-piece rudder

elevons

payload bay

crew compartment

carbon fiber nose cone

Wheels, Windows, and Hatches

● The orbiter has wheels so that it can land at the end of a mission. There are main wheels under each wing and a nose wheel.

● The crew compartment has windows so that the crew can see outside.

● The windows don't open because the air the crew need to breathe would escape into space.

● The astronauts go in and out of the crew compartment through a door called a hatch.

Main wheels under wing

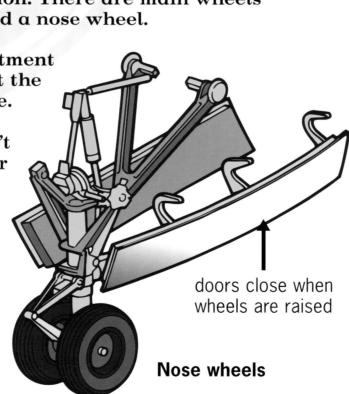

doors close when wheels are raised

Nose wheels

Fact Box
The orbiter can't use its engines for landing. The pilot must land perfectly the first time because he cannot try again.

Windows

The flight deck has six windows at the front, two in the roof, and two at the back.

window frame

roof windows

glass

front windows

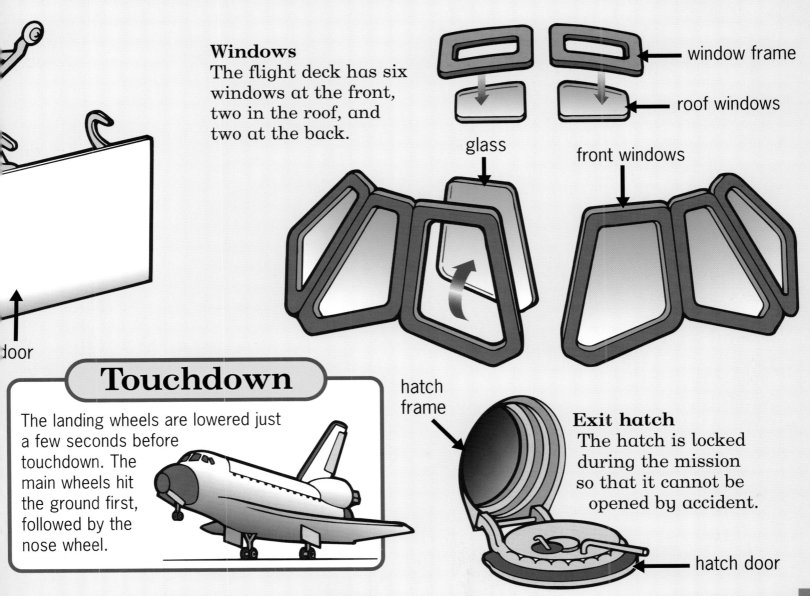

hatch frame

Touchdown

The landing wheels are lowered just a few seconds before touchdown. The main wheels hit the ground first, followed by the nose wheel.

Exit hatch

The hatch is locked during the mission so that it cannot be opened by accident.

hatch door

door

The Engines

- The orbiter has three different types of rocket engines.

- Three main engines, called SSMEs, help launch the shuttle into space.

- There are also two small engines called OMS engines.

- Mini engines called thrusters make the orbiter move about when it is in space.

Fact Box
Each of the orbiter's three main rocket engines is seven times as powerful as a jumbo jet engine.

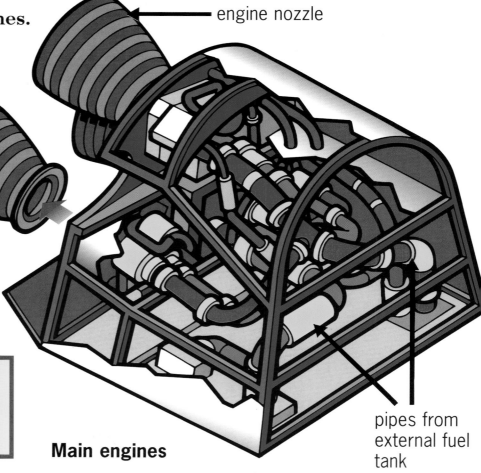

engine nozzle

engine nozzle

pipes from external fuel tank

Main engines

fuel tanks

rear
thrusters

OMS engine

Fuel tanks

Fuel for the OMS
engines and thrusters is
stored in tanks. There are
two different types of fuel.
When they mix together,
they explode, making a
stream of hot gas, which
drives the orbiter forward.

Thrusters

There are 44
thrusters in the
nose and tail.
They make the
orbiter turn and
roll, or move its
nose up or down.

thrusters

fuel tanks

nose

1 The orbiter can slow
down as well as speed
up using the OMS
engines.

2 To slow down, the
orbiter first turns
around using its
thrusters so
that it faces
backward.

3 Then it fires the
OMS engines. The
orbiter must slow
down to get
back to Earth.

Tanks and Boosters

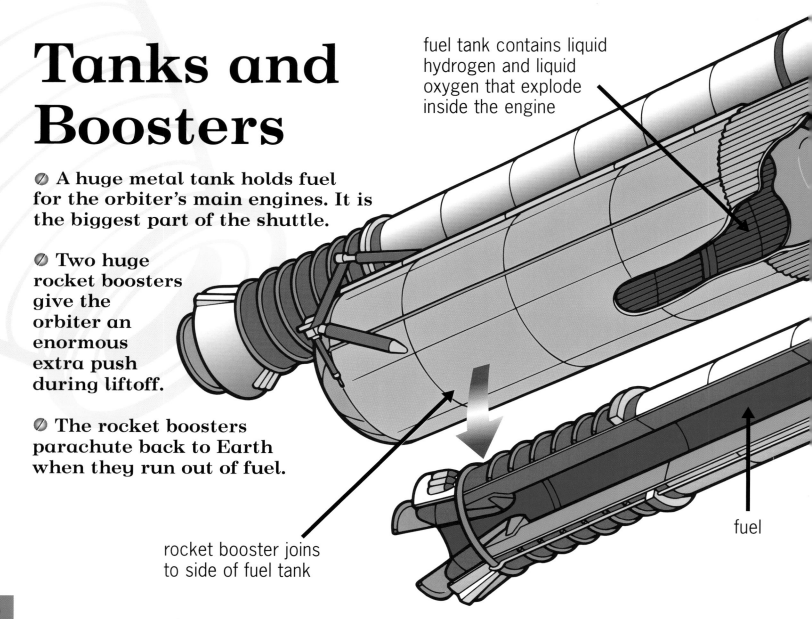

⊘ **A huge metal tank holds fuel for the orbiter's main engines. It is the biggest part of the shuttle.**

⊘ **Two huge rocket boosters give the orbiter an enormous extra push during liftoff.**

⊘ **The rocket boosters parachute back to Earth when they run out of fuel.**

fuel tank contains liquid hydrogen and liquid oxygen that explode inside the engine

fuel

rocket booster joins to side of fuel tank

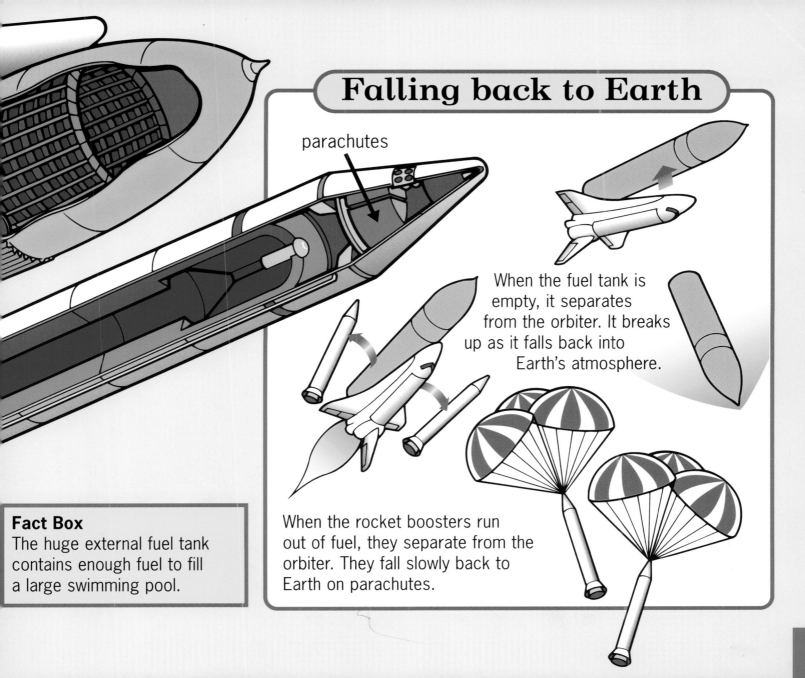

parachutes

Falling back to Earth

When the fuel tank is empty, it separates from the orbiter. It breaks up as it falls back into Earth's atmosphere.

When the rocket boosters run out of fuel, they separate from the orbiter. They fall slowly back to Earth on parachutes.

Fact Box
The huge external fuel tank contains enough fuel to fill a large swimming pool.

The Flight Deck

● **The commander and pilot control the shuttle from the flight deck.**

● **The flight deck is on the upper deck of the crew compartment.**

● **The pilot and commander are surrounded by panels with hundreds of switches, dials, and buttons.**

Fact Box
The shuttle has five computers. If the computers come up with different solutions to a problem, they "vote" to choose one.

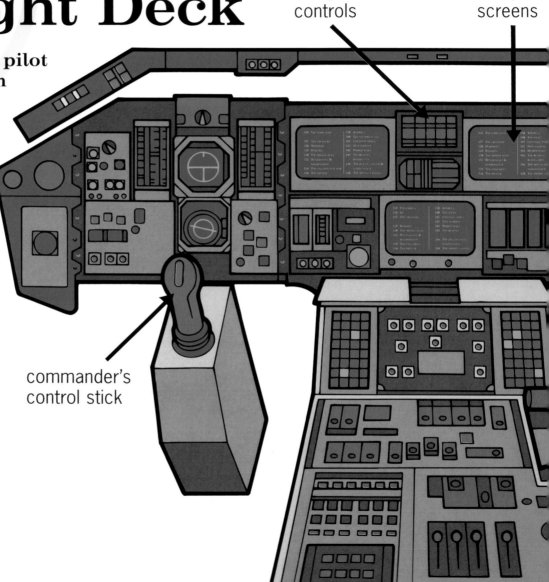

computer controls

compute screens

commander's control stick

flying instruments

pilot's control stick

seat belt

Payload controls

At the back of the flight deck is the crew station. There are controls here for the equipment in the payload bay and for the robot arm.

Don't move
A platform with foot straps keeps the operator from floating about.

head rest

Safe seats
All the crew members are safely strapped into seats for liftoff, reentry, and landing. The seats fold away when the orbiter is in space.

The Living Quarters

⦿ The living quarters are in the middeck of the crew compartment. They are filled with air so that the crew can breathe.

⦿ The living quarters contain bunks, a galley (like a kitchen), a toilet, and a sink.

⦿ A ladder leads from the middeck to the flight deck.

⦿ There is a utility area under the floor.

Fact Box
Astronauts come back to Earth up to 2 inches taller than when they left.

Lockers
At the front of the middeck is a wall of lockers. The locker drawers have foam rubber inside to keep things from floating about.

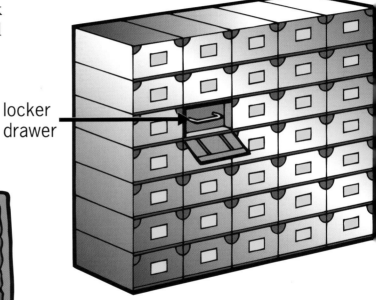

locker drawer

Medical supplies
The shuttle medical kit contains band-aids, bandages, and other equipment to help ill crew members until they can get back to Earth.

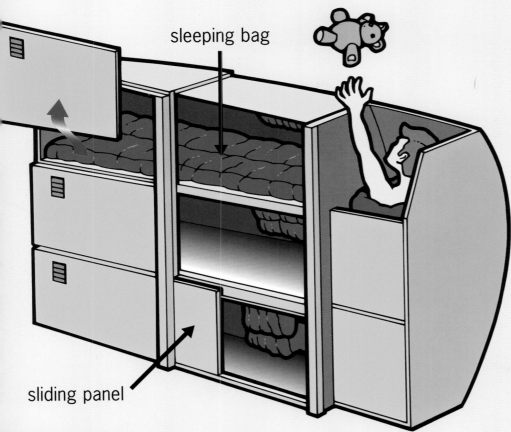

sleeping bag

sliding panel

Going to sleep

There are four bunks called sleep stations. Each one has a sleeping bag attached, which zips up to keep the astronaut from floating about. It doesn't matter which way up the astronauts sleep because they are weightless!

Keeping in shape

Astronauts have to exercise for about 15 minutes each day to keep their muscles and hearts healthy. The space shuttle carries a treadmill for this.

elastic straps pull astronaut down

Eating and Drinking

◉ **Opposite the sleep stations is a galley where the astronauts prepare their food and drink.**

◉ **The crew wash, using a small sink. There's no bath or shower.**

◉ **In the corner of the middeck is a toilet called the waste collection system.**

Fact Box
In space, crumbly foods, such as biscuits, have to be moistened to keep the crumbs from flying about.

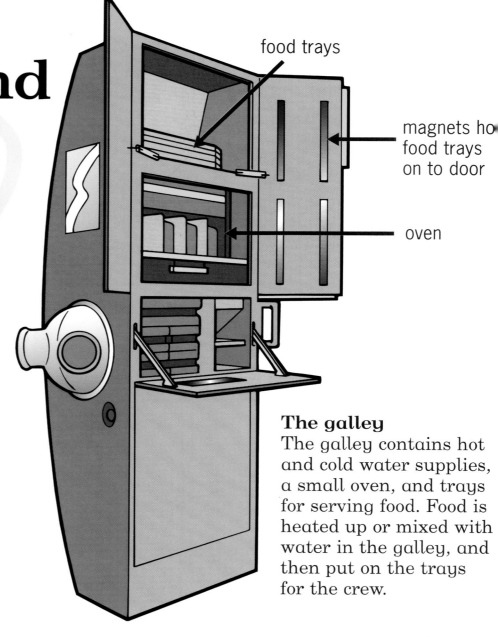

food trays

magnets ho
food trays
on to door

oven

The galley
The galley contains hot and cold water supplies, a small oven, and trays for serving food. Food is heated up or mixed with water in the galley, and then put on the trays for the crew.

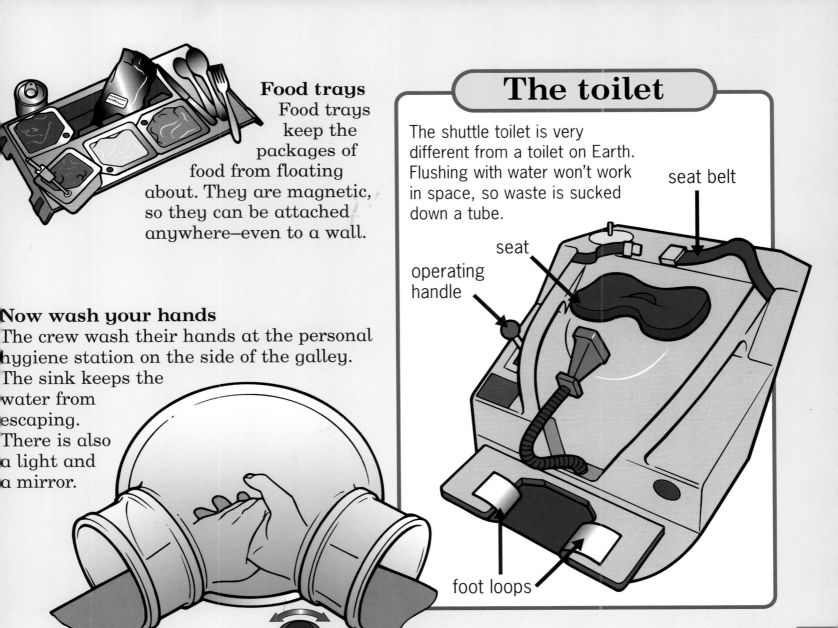

Food trays

Food trays keep the packages of food from floating about. They are magnetic, so they can be attached anywhere—even to a wall.

Now wash your hands

The crew wash their hands at the personal hygiene station on the side of the galley. The sink keeps the water from escaping. There is also a light and a mirror.

The toilet

The shuttle toilet is very different from a toilet on Earth. Flushing with water won't work in space, so waste is sucked down a tube.

seat belt

seat

operating handle

foot loops

Inside the Payload Bay

⊘ **The payload bay is inside the orbiter. It is where the shuttle's cargo is stored.**

⊘ **On some missions the cargo is a satellite that will be launched into space.**

⊘ **Some satellites are carried on top of a satellite launching cradle.**

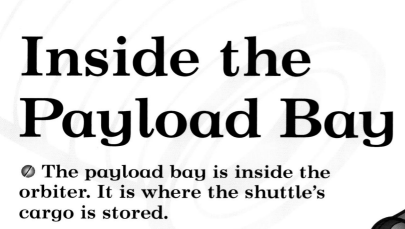

satellite

payload assist module fires satellite into higher orbit

spin table makes satellites spin around

satellite launching cradle

Fact Box
The payload bay is 60 feet long and 15 feet across. It's big enough to hold a large tour bus.

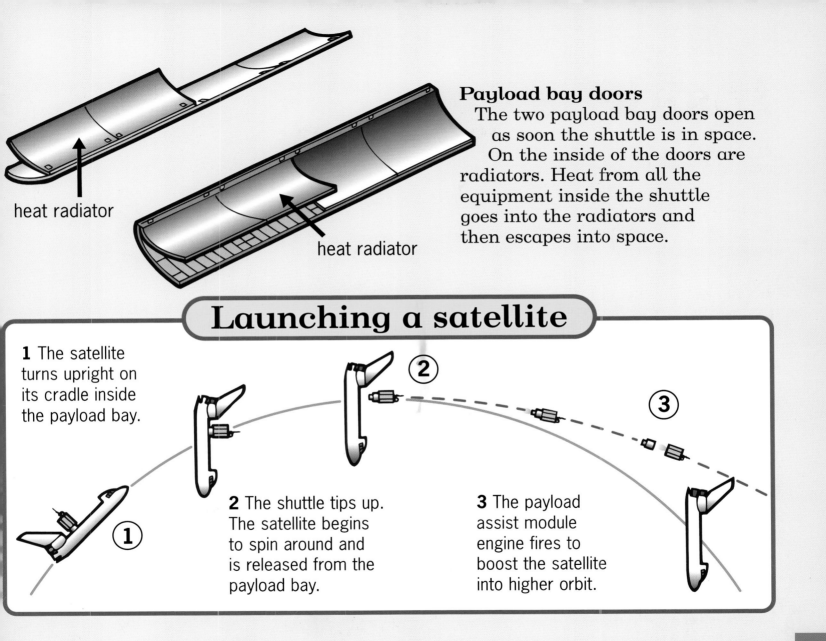

Payload bay doors
The two payload bay doors open as soon the shuttle is in space. On the inside of the doors are radiators. Heat from all the equipment inside the shuttle goes into the radiators and then escapes into space.

heat radiator

heat radiator

Launching a satellite

1 The satellite turns upright on its cradle inside the payload bay.

①

②

③

2 The shuttle tips up. The satellite begins to spin around and is released from the payload bay.

3 The payload assist module engine fires to boost the satellite into higher orbit.

Spacelab

⊘ Spacelab is a science laboratory that the shuttle can carry into orbit. It fits inside the payload bay.

⊘ Along the walls of Spacelab are bays containing experiments.

⊘ The crew crawl through the crew transfer tunnel to get from the crew compartment to Spacelab.

crew module

crew transfer tunnel

experiment bays

Fact Box
The crew is made up of the pilots who fly the shuttle and scientists, called mission specialists, who do experiments or launch satellites.

Mung beans

These beans were grown in Spacelab. Because the beans were weightless, the roots didn't know which way to grow.

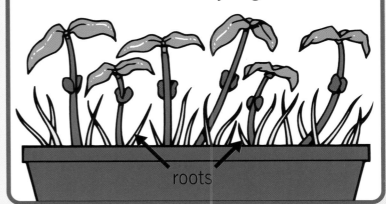

roots

Experiment platforms
Some experiments need to be carried out in open space instead of inside Spacelab. They are attached to special platforms that fit inside the payload bay behind Spacelab.

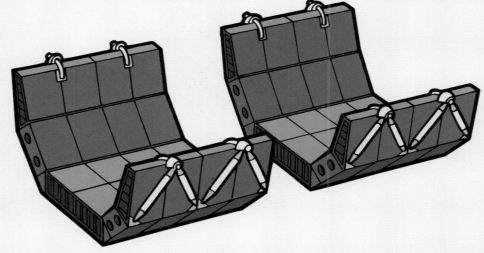

The Robot Arm

- The shuttle has a robot arm called the remote manipulator system (RMS for short).

- The arm can move satellites into and out of the payload bay.

- The arm has joints, so it can bend– just like your arm.

- At the end of the arm is a tool that can grab objects.

Control panel
A crew member controls the robot arm with a joystick and switches on the control panel of the rear flight deck. He or she can see the arm through the window.

Fact Box
Astronauts sometimes stand on a platform at the end of the robot arm when they are repairing a satellite.

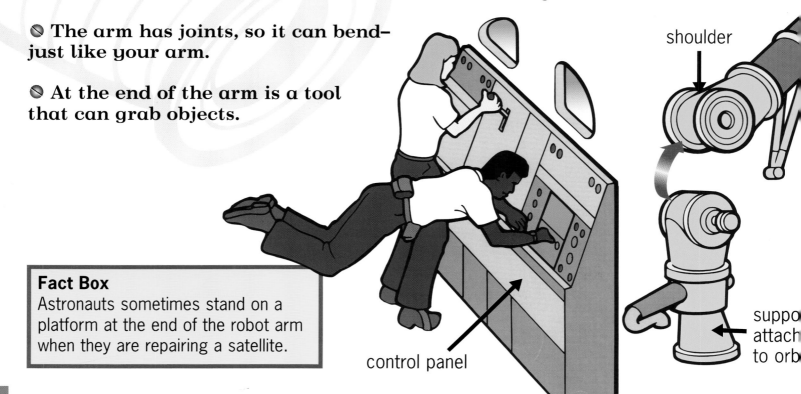

shoulder

control panel

suppo
attach
to orb

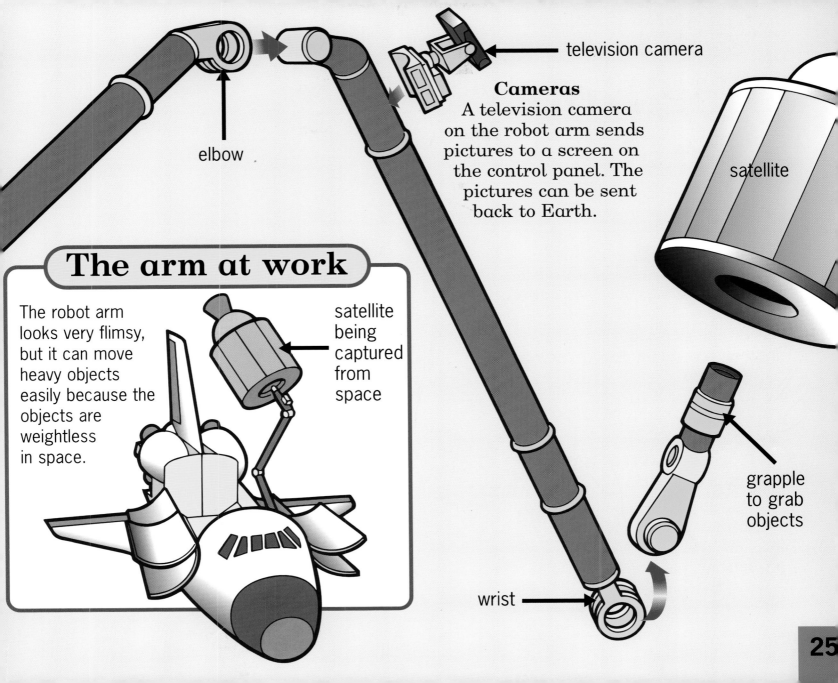

television camera

Cameras
A television camera on the robot arm sends pictures to a screen on the control panel. The pictures can be sent back to Earth.

satellite

elbow

The arm at work

The robot arm looks very flimsy, but it can move heavy objects easily because the objects are weightless in space.

satellite being captured from space

grapple to grab objects

wrist

Working Outside

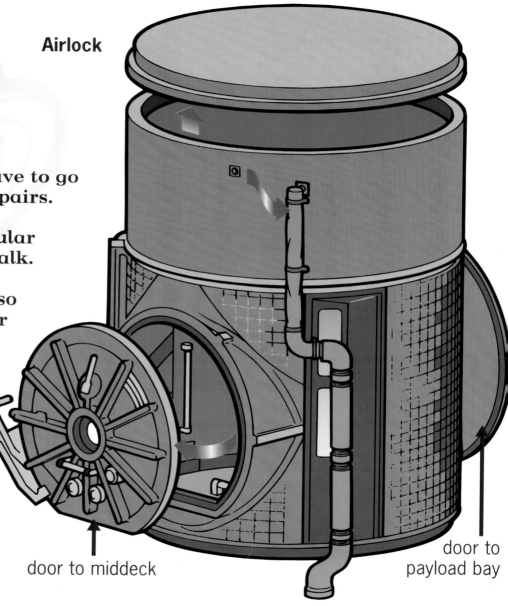

● Astronauts sometimes have to go outside the orbiter to do repairs.

⊘ This is called extravehicular activity (EVA), or a spacewalk.

⊘ There is no air in space, so the astronauts have to wear a spacesuit that contains a supply of oxygen.

● To get into space, the astronauts go through a room called the airlock.

Fact Box
A spacesuit is big and bulky. With all its parts, it weighs about 260 pounds.

door to middeck

door to payload bay

26

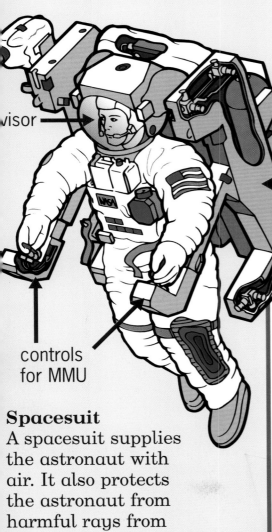

visor

controls
for MMU

Spacesuit

A spacesuit supplies
the astronaut with
air. It also protects
the astronaut from
harmful rays from
the sun and tiny rocks
that whizz through
space at high speed.

Moving about in space

Sometimes an astronaut wears a manned
maneuvering unit (MMU). It has tiny thrusters
that move the astronaut around in space.

MMU

How the airlock works

1 The astronaut opens the
inner hatch from the middeck
and climbs into the airlock. He
closes the hatch behind him.

2 The astronaut wriggles
carefully into his spacesuit.

He presses a button to let the
air out of the airlock.

3 After about three minutes
he can open the outer hatch.
He climbs out into the payload
bay and begins his spacewalk.

Ready to Launch

- Many weeks of preparation are needed before a shuttle is launched.

- First, equipment is loaded into the payload bay.

- Then the orbiter is attached to the external tank and rocket boosters.

- The shuttle is moved to the launch pad, and fuel is pumped into the tank.

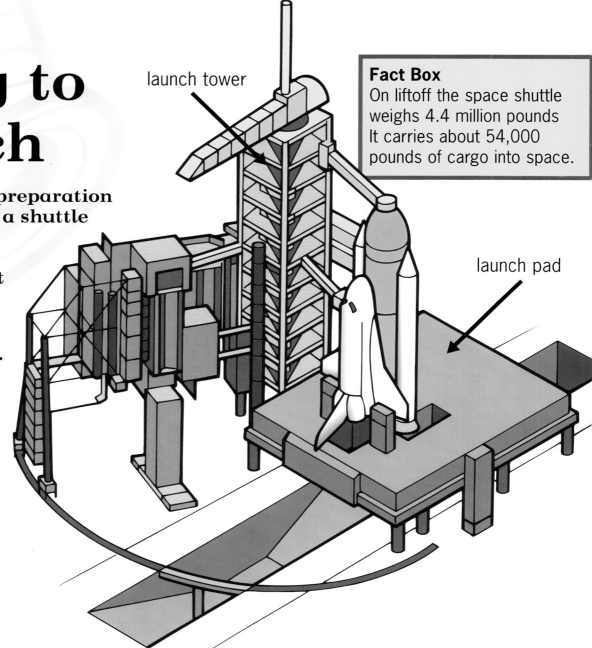

launch tower

launch pad

Fact Box
On liftoff the space shuttle weighs 4.4 million pounds It carries about 54,000 pounds of cargo into space.

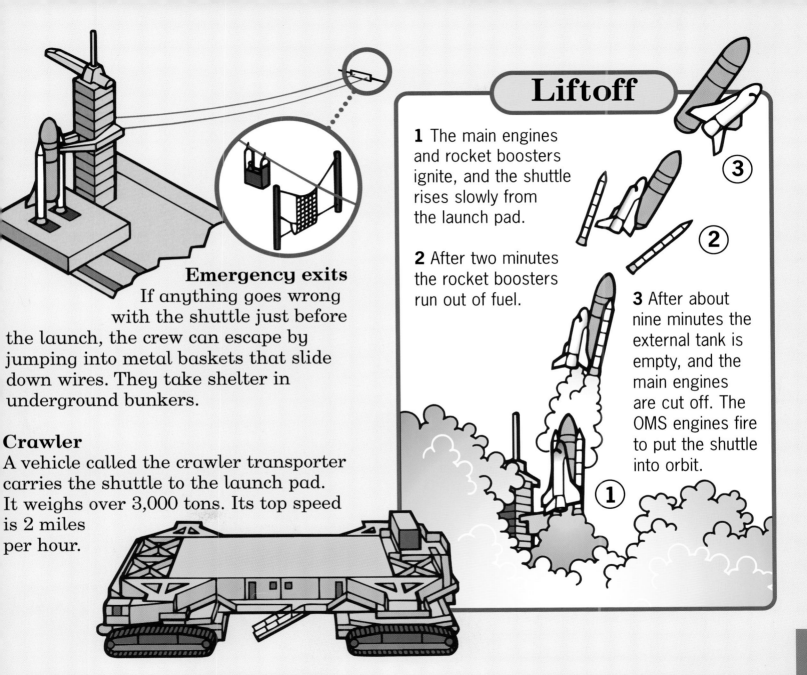

Emergency exits
If anything goes wrong with the shuttle just before the launch, the crew can escape by jumping into metal baskets that slide down wires. They take shelter in underground bunkers.

Crawler
A vehicle called the crawler transporter carries the shuttle to the launch pad. It weighs over 3,000 tons. Its top speed is 2 miles per hour.

Liftoff

1 The main engines and rocket boosters ignite, and the shuttle rises slowly from the launch pad.

2 After two minutes the rocket boosters run out of fuel.

3 After about nine minutes the external tank is empty, and the main engines are cut off. The OMS engines fire to put the shuttle into orbit.

③

②

①

Useful Words

airlock A small room that astronauts go through to get from their spacecraft into space.

atmosphere The thick blanket of air that surrounds Earth.

carbon fiber A material made from strands of carbon. It is stronger than steel and difficult to melt.

ceramic A material made from clay or sand, such as pottery or glass.

docking Linking up to another spacecraft in space so that crew can move from one spacecraft to another.

elevons Small flaps on the back of the orbiter's wings that the pilot moves to steer the orbiter back to Earth.

flight deck The control center of the shuttle.

hydrogen A gas that explodes when it is ignited.

ignite To make something start to burn.

joystick A small stick that moves backward and forward and from side to side. It is used to control a machine.

mission A trip into space to do a certain job.

orbit The huge circle that a spacecraft or satellite travels in around Earth. The space shuttle orbits just outside Earth's atmosphere.

oxygen A gas found in the atmosphere that we need in order to breathe. Oxygen is also needed to make things burn or explode. The space shuttle carries oxygen to make its hydrogen fuel burn.

payload Anything that the shuttle carries into space, such as a satellite or an experiment.

payload assist module A small rocket that carries a satellite away from the orbiter into a higher orbit.

radiators Panels that give off heat.

reentry The return of a spacecraft into Earth's atmosphere.

ribs Metal hoops that make up the orbiter's structure. They go around the orbiter.

rudder A flap on the back of the tail that the pilot moves to steer the orbiter as it glides back to Earth.

satellite A craft that orbits Earth. Some satellites take photographs of Earth, some pass on telephone calls and television pictures, and some investigate space.

spars Metal bars that make up the orbiter's structure. They go along the orbiter.

spin table A machine that makes a satellite spin around before it is launched into space. Spinning a satellite keeps it from wobbling about as it orbits Earth.

treadmill A machine like a moving pavement that the astronauts use to walk or run along when exercising.

weightlessness The feeling that there is no gravity, which makes an astronaut float about. Astronauts feel weightless as they orbit Earth.

Index

air 8, 16, 26, 27
airlock 26, 27, 30
astronauts 8, 16-18,
  24, 26, 27
atmosphere 11, 13,
  30

commander 14
computers 14
crawler transporter
  29
crew 6, 8, 15, 16,
  18, 22, 29
crew compartment
  5, 7, 8, 14, 16, 22

Earth 6, 7, 11-13,
  16, 19, 25

eating 16, 18, 19
elevons 6, 7, 30
engines 5, 8, 10,
  11, 12, 29
exercising 17
external fuel tank
  4, 10, 12, 13, 28, 29

flight deck 9, 14-16,
  24, 30
fuel 11-13, 28-29

hatches 8, 9, 27

landing 4, 8, 9, 11,
  15
launch pad 4, 28, 29
liftoff 4, 10, 12, 15,
  28, 29
lockers 16

MMU 27

nose cone 4, 7

orbiter 4-8, 10-13,
  15, 20, 24, 26, 28

parachutes 12, 13
payload 6, 30
payload bay 5, 7,
  15, 20-24, 27, 28
pilot 7, 8, 14, 22

radiators 21, 31
reentry 7, 11, 15,
  31
ribs 6, 31
robot arm 5, 15, 24,
  25
rocket boosters 4, 5,
  12, 13, 28, 29
rudder 5-7, 31

satellites 20-22, 24,
  25, 31
seats 15
sleeping 16-17
Spacelab 22, 23
spacesuits 26, 27
spacewalk 26, 27
spars 6, 31

tail 5-7, 11
thrusters 10, 11
tiles 6, 7
toilet 16, 18, 19

washing 18, 19
weightlessness 15-19
  23, 25, 31
wheels 8
windows 8, 9, 24
wings 5-8

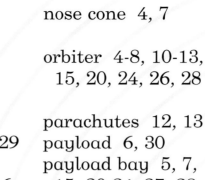